How to Use This Book

The **Teaching Versions** of *Elements of Reading: Fluency* will help you guide children to become fluent readers. Because fluency is not an isolated skill but is closely linked to word knowledge and comprehension, each **Teaching Version** contains the following types of teacher support:

- **Fluency teaching suggestions** to help children become proficient in reading with expression (prosody).
- **Word knowledge teaching suggestions** to build children's proficiency in reading words and understanding their structure and meanings. The word knowledge suggestions address recognition of high-frequency words, decoding skills, structural analysis skills, and knowledge of word meanings.
- **Sen**
que
literal comprehension at the sentence level.
- **Text comprehension questions** to help children develop inferential comprehension. Additional comprehension questions are provided in the **Teacher's Lesson Folder.**

After children have completed the repeated reading activities outlined on page 5.12 of the **Teacher's Lesson Folder,** use the reduced **Student Book** pages and teaching suggestions in this **Teaching Version** to provide explicit page-by-page instruction.

Dogs That Help Us

Fluency Focus

Expression Using stress to convey meaning

Punctuation Observing junctures indicated by periods

Text Format Reading headings

Word Knowledge Focus

Decoding Words with short *e*

Theme High-Frequency Words (Boldface words appear in each book of the theme.)

a, about, air, and, are, by, can, day, every, **find**, follow, for, get, good, have, hear, help, how, in, is, it, its, keep, **let's**, many, of, on, out, people, see, some, sometimes, **still**, take, the, their, **then**, they, to, too, use, well, **what**, who

Sentence Comprehension Focus

Comprehending stated details

Text Comprehension Focus

Classifying

Dogs That Help Us

Written by Claire Llewellyn

Harcourt Achieve
Rigby • Saxon • Steck-Vaughn

www.HarcourtAchieve.com
1.800.531.5015

Getting Started

To begin, invite a volunteer to read the title page aloud.

Book Summary

This nonfiction book answers the question *How do dogs help us?* Three types of helping dogs are presented—guide dogs, hearing dogs, and search dogs. Readers learn that a dog's senses can help people in need.

Fluency

Read the sentences on the page aloud, stressing the boldface words below. Have children listen for the words that are stressed. Point out that stressing words helps a listener and the reader understand the book.

Dogs have good **senses.**
They can **see, hear,** and **smell** well.

Word Knowledge

Direct children's attention to the words "senses," "smell," and "well." Write the words on the board. Ask what vowel sound they hear in each word (short *e*). Point out that the letter *e* stands for the short *e* sound. Circle the letter in both words.

Dogs have good senses.
They can see, hear, and smell well.

2

Sentence Comprehension

Ask *What can dogs do well?* (see, hear, and smell)

A dog's senses can help people.
Let's find out how.

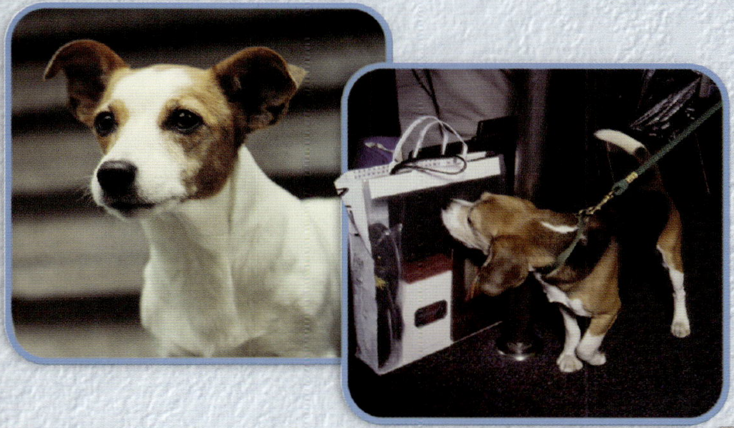

3

■ **Sentence Comprehension**

Ask *What do dogs use to help people?* (their senses)

■ **Fluency**

Have children read the page silently to decide which words should be stressed. Have volunteers share their opinions and their reading of the page. Children should stress the boldface words below:

A dog's **senses** can **help** people.
Let's find out **how**.

Ask children where they should pause on pages 2–3 (after each sentence).

■ **Word Knowledge**

Have children write the theme high-frequency words (*find*, *let's*, *still*, *then*, *what*) on small self-stick notes.

Have children identify the theme high-frequency words on the page and place the corresponding self-stick note by each.

Fluency

Lead children in a discussion of the words that should be stressed on the page. Use the following boldface words as a guide:

Let's **Find Out** About **Guide** Dogs

Some dogs help people who cannot **see.** They are called **guide** dogs.

Point out the heading at the top of the page. Ask children what they should do after a heading (pause). Lead children in an echo reading of the page.

Word Knowledge

Have children identify the theme high-frequency words on the page and place the correct self-stick note by each.

Have children find the short *e* words on the page ("Let's," "help"). Add "help" to the list of short *e* words.

Let's Find Out About Guide Dogs

Some dogs help people who cannot see.
They are called guide dogs.

4

Sentence Comprehension

Ask *What are dogs that help people who cannot see called?* (guide dogs)

Guide dogs see for their owner. They take their owner outside. They help their owner cross the street.

■ Fluency

Read the page in a monotone, without pausing at the ends of sentences. Ask children how your reading should change to be fluent. Have children implement their suggestions about stressing particular words and pausing at the ends of sentences as they read the page in unison.

■ Sentence Comprehension

Ask *Where do guide dogs take their owner?* (outside)

Fluency

Guide children to arrive at a consensus on which words should be stressed in a fluent reading of the page. Remind them that stressed words help a listener and reader understand what they are reading.

Word Knowledge

Read the page aloud. Have children raise their hand when they hear a theme high-frequency word.

A guide dog helps its owner every day.
It sees what its owner cannot see.

6

Sentence Comprehension

Ask *How does a guide dog help its owner?* (It sees things its owner cannot.)

Fluency

Point out that since the page tells what a guide dog does, it is important to stress words that tell what the dog does, along with other important words. Have children decide which words should be stressed on the page and demonstrate stressing them.

Ask children to scan page 7 and tell how many sentences are there (two). Have children explain how they know. (There are two periods.) Ask children what fluent readers do when they come to a period (pause).

Sentence Comprehension

Ask *Why does a guide dog guide its owner?* (to keep the owner safe)

Fluency

Begin reading page 8 with the first sentence, omitting the heading. Stop and ask children if this is where you should have begun. Reread the page, beginning with the heading. As you read, be sure to stress the words "hearing" and "hear." Invite children to explain why it is important to emphasize those words. Invite children to read the page aloud together.

Word Knowledge

Have a volunteer read the page aloud. Ask children to raise their hand when they hear a theme high-frequency word.

Let's Find Out About Hearing Dogs

Some dogs help people who cannot hear.
They are called hearing dogs.

8

Sentence Comprehension

Ask *What are dogs that help people who cannot hear called?* (hearing dogs)

Hearing dogs hear sounds for their owner.
They see what makes the sounds.

9

■ **Sentence Comprehension**

Ask *What do hearing dogs do for their owner?* (hear sounds and see what makes them)

■ **Fluency**

Read the page without pausing at the first period. Ask children whether you read the page well. Invite a volunteer to read the page correctly.

Fluency

As you read the sentences on this page, make sure that you read at an appropriate pace. Remind children that fluent readers always make their reading sound like talking, including stressing important words and pausing at the end of sentences. Lead children in an echo reading of the page.

Word Knowledge

Read the page aloud. Have children hold up the self-stick note for the high-frequency word that appears on the page.

A hearing dog helps its owner every day.
It hears what its owner cannot hear.

10

Sentence Comprehension

Ask *What does a hearing dog do when the phone rings?* (It tells its owner.)

Fluency

Explain to children that sometimes readers stress some words to help indicate an order of events. Read the second sentence aloud, stressing the word "Then." Ask children which word was said with extra force to indicate order of events. Have them join you in reading page 11 aloud.

Word Knowledge

Refer children to the list of short *e* words on the board. Ask children if the theme high-frequency word *then* belongs with the words (yes). Have a volunteer add *then* to the list.

Have children find the other short *e* word on the page (tells). Add *tells* to the list.

Fluency

Have children read the page silently to decide which words should be stressed. Have children share their opinions. Use the following as a guide for the page:

Let's **Find Out** About **Search** Dogs

Some dogs find **people** who are **lost.** They are called **search** dogs.

Read the page aloud, stopping after each pause to ask children to explain why you paused there.

Word Knowledge

Have children identify the theme high-frequency words that appear on the page and place the correct self-stick note by each.

Let's Find Out About Search Dogs

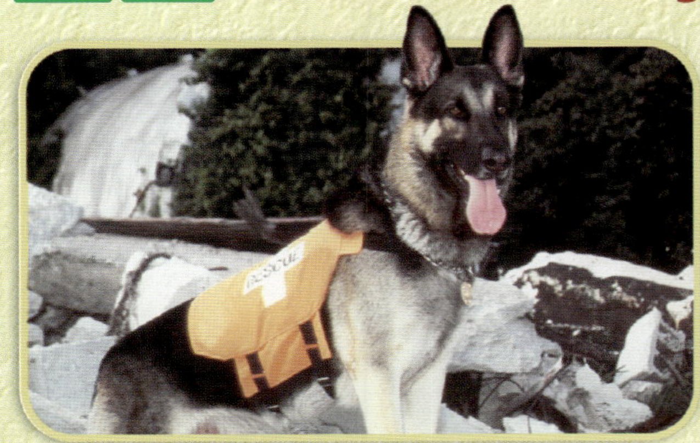

Some dogs find people who are lost.
They are called search dogs.

12

Sentence Comprehension

Ask *What are dogs that find lost people called?* (search dogs)

Search dogs use their sense of smell.
They smell the air and the ground.
They follow smells.

13

■ Sentence Comprehension

Ask *What do search dogs do when they find smells?* (follow them)

■ Fluency

Ask children what they can do to help a listener notice important words. (They can stress the words.) Have children read the page in unison. Encourage them to make their reading sound like talking and to emphasize important words.

■ Word Knowledge

Call attention to the word "smell." Add it to the list of short *e* words on the board. Read the words in the list, asking children to listen for the vowel sound in each word. Have a volunteer circle the letter that stands for the vowel sound in "sense" and "smell" (*e*).

Fluency

Ask children to read the page silently and think about which words need to be stressed. Have volunteers share their opinion. Lead children in a choral reading of the page. Afterward, have children tell how they knew where to pause.

Word Knowledge

Have children identify the theme high-frequency word on the page and place the correct self-stick note under its first use.

Call attention to the word "get." Ask children to tell whether this word belongs in the list of short *e* words on the board and to explain why or why not. Have a volunteer add the word to the list on the board and circle the letter that stands for the short *e* sound.

Sometimes people get lost.
Their smell is still in the air.
It is still on the ground.

14

Sentence Comprehension

Ask *Where does a search dog find a lost person's smell?* (in the air and on the ground)

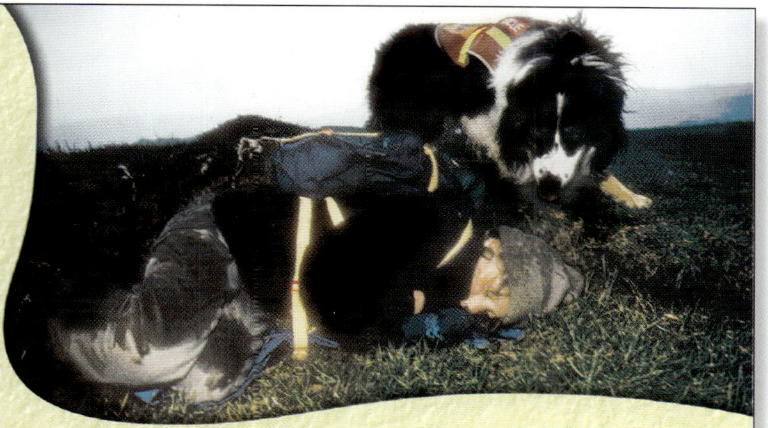

A search dog finds the smell.
Then it follows the smell.
It finds the people who are lost.

15

Fluency

Read the page as one continuous sentence with no pauses. Ask children if the reading made sense to them and have them tell what was incorrect about the reading. Have the group read the page together.

Sentence Comprehension

Ask *What happens after the search dog follows the smell?* (It finds the people who are lost.)

Fluency

Point out the exclamation mark at the end of the last sentence. Invite children to read along with you in a choral reading of the page. Have children identify the words they stressed.

Dogs Help Us

Dogs help many people.
They are good friends to people, too!

16

Sentence Comprehension

Ask *What do dogs do besides help people?* (They are good friends to people, too.)

Text Comprehension

Ask *Which dogs help people who cannot hear?* (hearing dogs)

Ask *Which dogs help people who cannot see?* (guide dogs)

Ask *Which dogs help find lost people?* (search dogs)

Ask *What would be a good name for the group that includes hearing dogs, guide dogs, and search dogs?* (Answers will vary; you may wish to tell children about the term "service dogs.")

Fluency Flip Page

The **Fluency Flip Page** of the **Student Book** contains a passage from the book to facilitate timed reading. For more information on timed reading and other ways of assessing fluency, see the **Teacher's Lesson Folder.**

Let's Find Out About Search Dogs 6

Some dogs find people who are lost. 13

They are called search dogs. 18

Search dogs use their sense of smell. 25

They smell the air and the ground. 32

They follow smells. 35

Sometimes people get lost. 39

Their smell is still in the air. 46

It is still on the ground. 52

A search dog finds the smell. 58

Then it follows the smell. 63

It finds the people who are lost. 70

Dogs Help Us 73

Dogs help many people. 77

They are good friends to people, too! 84